MW01198922

EMPTY
A pilgrim's memoir

Published by MTPages
3514 Corondo Ct. Houston, Texas 77005, USA

Copyright©Patrick J. Miller, 2009 All rights reserved

New Revised Standard Version Bible, copyright© 1989, Division of Christian
Education of the National Council of the Churches of Christ in the United
States of America. Used by permission. All rights reserved.

ISBN 1448678307

EAN 13 9781448678303

Without limiting the rights under copyright reserved above, no part of this
publication may be reproduced, stored in or introduced into a retrieval system,
or transmitted, in any form or by any means (electronic, mechanical,
photocopying, recording or otherwise), without the prior written consent of
the author.

The scanning, uploading, and distribution of this book via the Internet or via
any other means without the permission of the author is illegal and punishable
by law. Please purchase only authorized electronic editions and do not
participate in or encourage electronic piracy of copyrighted materials. Your
support of the author's rights is appreciated.

Cover designed by Jill Knobloch

Cover photo— Candleholder, upper room of St. Mark's
Syrian Orthodox Church, Jerusalem, by Patrick J. Miller.

In memory of Keri, Elizabeth, and Kelly

Contents

Introduction: Being Full

I.   Salem

II.   Normal

III.   Doors

IV.   The Sea of Galilee

V.   Siege

VI.   Pawn Shops

VII.   Justina

VIII.   Graves

IX.   Women of the Resurrection

X.   Emmaus

Epilogue: Being Empty

Empty

A pilgrim's memoir

Patrick J. Miller

Introduction

Being Full

One time I had to pick a monk up at the airport. While we drove we struck up pleasant conversation: who we were, where we were from, our parents, life. I asked what he did for the monastery, and he described his work and his life. From his description he sounded busy. I described my work and life to him. I also sounded busy. After a while I said, "Wow! We are both pretty busy." To which he replied, "Well, yes, but monks like to say our lives are full." I liked that notion of full. Lives are full. Busy is noise. We can be busy but never full, never satisfied. Full means something more. Leave it to the monks to once again dispense wisdom with a single word.

When I think about it, being full has its dark side. Full can also lead to obesity. We are an obese society in many ways. Our physical size aside, we have full, obese lives. We fill our days with hour to hour to hour appointments. We work seventy, eighty, even a hundred hours a week. We have children, parents, social obligations that fill our attention. We have full <u>and</u> busy lives. This kind of life is one we chose, an act of will. We live in a free society. No one told us we had to pick up an extra shift, or go to law school or medical school or business school. Sometimes financial obligations demand we work hard, but no one held a gun to our head and demanded that we earn a certain income and live in a certain house at a certain price. No one demanded that we fill our days with committee work and meetings. For most of us, we chose to. We chose the road and we chose to pay the toll. Somewhere along the way we found we could not get off our chosen path. Life was too full. The demands were often overwhelming. We began to do many things but none of them well. We tried to rewire the system, take a vacation, change jobs, something to un-fill the very full existence we had made.

In the winter of 2006 I found myself at the age of forty. In 2008 I found myself in charge of a congregation of people and chairman of a school board. My wife's own career was beginning to accelerate. Our children were growing fast. We were living a full life at a busy pace. Late night meetings were the new normal. We created a term "the go back" which described our going back to the office, sometimes until 1:00AM. We are both committed people. If we say we will do something, we will do it. I said I would be a husband, father, priest, and I would assume all of the responsibilities and duties that come with those committments. All three of my choices required public statements— at my wedding, my ordination, and the baptism of my children. I had created a full life for myself. And I was drowning in the full life I had made.

I was full, but I was not satisfied. I was full, but I was exhausted. I was full of life, but I was beginning to overdose on it. My life was full but full of noise. My life was filled up, and I was unable to add anything more. It was not what the monk had in mind. A full life for me meant being oversaturated to the point that I was no good to anyone. I exhibited all of the signs of trouble. I was quick tempered, often depressed, self medicating, impatient with those closest to me, tired, angry. I was full.

It is with this fullness that I stepped onto an airplane and flew over to Israel. I had no idea what I would find there, whom I would meet, where I would be going, except that I needed to be in Jersualem at The College of St.

George by 6:00PM on a Monday. Once there, I began a two-week pilgrimage through the country. The following pages are reflections of my time there.

I believe the Christian life should be a full one, but not the kind of full I just described. The day-to-day obligations that we set up for ourselves lead us into a misleading fullness. Truly full lives are ones that see us full of patience, of love, of kindness, of joy. These are the things that our Christian teaching pushes us towards. We act on these attributes, not out of obligation, but out of a genuine spirit of God. We have met these people before. They have full lives too. The full lives that these people have are born from a spirit of God that I too often miss. I become blinded and need to have my eyesight restored. I need to be refilled.

Forty years old is often the turning point in the life journey. It is at this point that we stop and re-think and turn inward. My mentor, Pittman McGehee, says the first half of life is an exterior journey, and that the second half is an interior one. Lives full of noise block our ability to see our true Christian mission. I believe that in order to look inside of ourselves, to be full again, we must be empty first.

Full and empty are good themes for a pilgrim in the holy land. They are the opposite of what we think they mean. A full life can be an empty one. An empty life can be a full one. An empty life gives us a chance to fill ourselves with the grace of God. A full life can create a situation where there is no room for God. I was full and empty when I got to Israel. I was empty and full when I returned. Along the way I discovered that I must become empty in order to be transformed and ready for the second half of the journey. Empty becomes the goal of the Christian, at least for me anyway. Maybe it is the same for others.

The next few pages are my imperfect way to describe the places I visited and the ways I was emptied and filled. Ultimately we will all be empty of life, as we all will die. I believe we can find full lives before we die. I did.

I invite you to take the pilgrimage with me. See what you want to see in the words that follow. I invite you to an empty life that is full of potential and love. I invite you to remind yourself of wonder. In the fullness of time I hope that we are able to reclaim room for God. This room is an empty space with two chairs. A room full of conversation between the creator and the created. An empty room full.

I

Salem

About 2500 BCE someone walked up onto a hill about thirty miles from the Mediterranean Sea, near a stream, and a few miles from a river. He or she, no one knows which, walked up onto this hill looked around, and something happened. Something happened on that hill that made him or her say the word, "Salem" under their breath, or maybe to the people walking with them. "Salem" grew to mean "peace" and the hill grew to be known as Jerusalem, a city of peace. Over the next four thousand years that city of peace has straddled two points, peace and turbulence. Both occurred here. Both still seem possible here. Now it is 2009, peace is still here, turbulence still possible, and I am there for the first time.

I am not the first priest to walk around the old city and go through the motions of awe and wonder. I am not the first priest to make a pilgrimage of faith. I am not the first to come to "salem" and have my faith reinvigorated and my sense of vocation renewed. No, and I may even run the risk of being a cliché of sorts. Volumes have been printed on this city, on the faiths that occupy her, and the political regimes that each millennium ruled her over and again. What else can be said? A member of my group commented, "We have come to see what we have heard about all these years, see it with our own eyes and use our senses to get a full understanding of this city." That is what many say when they come here.

And why not be a cliché if it means that I get to visit where the holy collides with the creation. There is no risk then, only privilege, only blessing. My own eyes, my own soul, my own faith is joined with Melchizedek, King of Salem and priest of God most high. (Gen. 14.18). The first realization I have on this journey is to be reminded that the first act of the King of Salem was to offer hospitality to Abram. The first work of a priest is to offer hospitality. To me, a priest is ordained by the community to stand at the place where the holy collides with the creation, an altar of a church, a baptismal pool, a wedding rail, a deathbed. It is in these places where he or she offers hospitality in the bread and wine or the other sacraments. The priests are then called to take the things that human hands prepare and offer them up to God and then give them out to the people. Priests are to welcome the stranger to the table and remind everyone that God is near. Which is why "Salem" is not a place; it is not a temple. Salem is the living stones of the created. With each day God wakes me up with the sun and says, "Get up and go." I squint into the light and ask, "Go where?" God says, "Go." And I do, and suddenly I find myself being a living sacrifice, a part of the creative process of God. All I did was get up into another day of my life and go. Maybe it is the same for everyone who has a calling. One cannot help but go.

I believe priesthood is not the single act of one person. To be a priest you must have people to be a priest among. It takes a community of people to make a priest. That community must already have realized that they are a priesthood themselves. For me, God makes the people, the people make the community, the community makes the priest. It is with these thoughts that I am wandering around the Holy Land. I am an emissary from my community of St. Mark's. They have sent me here, encouraged me to go. They are looking out for my family while I am away. They are praying for me while I travel. It is they whom I serve, and it is they who make me a priest, and together we live into the faith that we have come to share.   Our priesthood then stands in line with Melchizedek. We each are Kings and Queens of Salem. We each strive to live out the call of another teacher who walked around in the streets of this city. We answered the call of a baptism into the ministry of Jesus of Nazareth. Our priesthood is found in that branch of the Holy One of Israel.

My first sight of the city was from the roof of the convent Maison d' Abraham overlooking the Mount of Olives. From this point I could scan the city. My eyes moved from the Mount of Olives, across the Kidron Valley to the Dome of the Rock, to the old steps into the Temple, to the archeological site of the City of David, and then across the Hinnom Valley and the Western Hill of the city. At one point fireworks went off, and they rose to about eye level with me on the roof. Fireworks in the middle of the day seemed odd. I noticed that the air where I stood smelled like Camp Allen, a pine tree smell, as the grounds of the convent are shaded by pines. I did not think anything profound—no "ah-ha" moments struck me.

I just stood there looking out at four thousand years of history. So many people have lived and died for this very small piece of real estate. Songs and poems, articles and novels, paintings and architecture, blood and tears, armies and zealots, the powerful and the powerless, humans at their best best and our humans at their worst have each been applied to the landscape that I was now seeing, hearing, smelling.

All I could think of is that it smelled like Camp Allen. And maybe that is the point.

Camp Allen is a camp and conference center in the piney woods of Texas. I went there as a child. My memories of safety and care there are deep. It was in that place that I discovered my faith. It was in that place that I found my calling as a priest. It is that place that I continue to retreat to when I am empty. Camp Allen is its own Salem. Camp Allen is a place that echoes the call of the faithful in the gift of hospitality. I learned how to be a Christian at Camp Allen. It is only fitting that in my first encounter with the

Holy City of God I should find a touchstone to the core of my faith.

There is a field in the back of the Camp Allen property. Near the edge of that field is a small, open area surrounded by pine trees. In that place, over twenty years ago, I stood and had an open-air conversation with God. It was a frank and honest conversation. I was struggling with the notion of vocation and what on earth I was to do with myself. I asked God to tell me what to do. No reply. I complained to God with a litany of words. No reply. I grew self-righteous and arrogant, spewing my case into the thin air. No reply. I became silent having exhausted my adolescent concerns. The silence grew and I stood there suddenly frozen, listening to it. There was no sound, maybe my heart beating, maybe me breathing. Then a wind grew through the tall pine trees, and I felt something, not dramatic, just something in the air, someone close, in my periphery. The wind blew and nothing was said but in my soul I heard, "peace." In the smell of the pine cones I heard, "peace." In some way, just like the person who walked up onto that hill in Jerusalem and said "peace," on that day I said it too.

They say there are thin places in the world, thin places where the creation meets the creator. Language is no good there. Neither is logic. In those places the soul is stirred. Memories of those places are unlocked by the simplest moments. A child crying. A song on the radio. A word from a loved one. A pew in a church. A hill in the desert. A field in a forest. In those moments of memory we regain something lost. We see ourselves again. We see why we started off on the journey in the first place. We remember why we fell in love. We are astounded that we are alive. We see God in the ordinary. We hear God in the silence.

Each of us are Kings and Queens of Salem. Our priesthood is found in the moments where we are silent. Our call is to hospitality, our lives given to service to each other. Our story is linked not by geography, but by blood and spirit. Each generation tells the story of a God who desires peace and a people who struggle to make that true. Each generation sends its own to Jerusalem, and in some way their own lives are re-tied to the promised land.

It smells like Camp Allen. It stirs the soul like that of an adolescent. It re-claims the faithful. It reminds the forgetful. It is truly a place of peace amid human frailty. It is the starting point of the God of our ancestors. It is the place we return to. It is the place where I am now. I am finding it is a place I will always strive to find forever. Salem. Shalom. Salaam.

II

Normal

My trip to Jeruslem was a two week pilgrimage with the College of St. George. I was among thirty-three people intent on studying the Palestine of Jesus. On the first day of the class I wandered into the old city of Jerusalem. I had four new friends with me. We were asked to discover the Islamic quarter. The old city of Jerusalem is divided into four quarters, Armenian, Christian, Jewish and Muslim. We gathered our cameras and bottled water and went.

As we made our way, members of our group commented that there are many Christian holy sites in the Muslim quarter. Along the narrow streets you will find the Via Delorosa, the traditional way of the cross. St. Anne's church, the traditional birthplace of Anne, the mother of Mary, is there. The pool where Jesus healed the blind man is on the grounds of St. Anne's. In one direction is the Mount of Olives, in the other is Mount Zion.

At the intersection of the Via Delorosa is Al Wad Street. Al Wad begins at the Damascus gate. If you follow Al Wad street you come to the western wall of the temple mount, commonly called the Wailing Wall. Our route took us in a circle, following the ramparts on the old wall, then down the Via Delorosa, then down Al Wad to the temple mount. We walked back up Al Wad to the Damascus gate and back to the college. We spent about six hours wandering around.

We entered the Muslim Quarter through Herod's Gate. We couldn't get our bearings, so we backtracked up to the Damascus Gate, and went down into an old Roman Gate, bought a ticket, and climbed up to the top of the ramparts. From there we could see the old city. We followed along the ramparts to a corner where in 1099 Godfrey of Bouillon breached the city walls and conquered the city. From this corner we got another view of the Mount of Olives and the gold onion domes of the Russian monastery that signals the Garden of Gethsemane. The day we climbed was the 910th anniversary of July 22, 1099, and a council Godfrey held in the Church of the Resurrection, home to the Holy Sepulchre, the domes of which could also be seen from where we were standing.

As we walked along I noticed the normalcy of the everyday. When walking the ramparts we were walking through the backyards of people's homes. We walked past schools and parks. We walked past one rooftop that had an old washing machine next to some old car doors and a car fender. I commented that the scene made me feel at home in small town Texas, the odd mix of salvaged items hanging around the yard. I could look up and see the gold dome of the temple mount. It was all rather surreal to me. I was struck by the history of the city and the reality of everyday living on display inside the city walls.

We climbed down the wall at St. Stephen's gate, which opens onto a road that leads out of the city to the Mount of Olives. We turned instead into the city; we were on the Via Delorosa. We wandered down that road to the intersection of Al Wad and stopped to have lunch.

Here is where the people watching began. We sat at a pizza restaurant. We were told the best pizza in town is made there. I ordered the ka-bob plate. We all ordered lemonades. I am not sure about the pizza, but the lemonade with crushed mint is religious. We saw everyone and everybody walking down Al Wad Street. The Austrian Hospice was across from us. Station III of the way of the cross, where Jesus falls for the first time, was in front of us. From our vantage point we witnessed the tourists, the Muslims, the Hasidics, the secular, the Christians, the Oklahomans, the French, the Greeks, the Arabs, the men and the women, the shop keepers, the boys who move goods around on carts. They were all moving in parade in front of us. It is a busy spot, and a good spot for us to sit and watch.

"I wonder," I said as we sat there, "if on that day, a couple of folks like us were just sitting here as a parade of criminals came by carrying wooden beams on their shoulders." There was general agreement. Someone chimed in, "The noise would pass by, and then they would return to their business." Someone else thought for a second, then added, "Nothing much to see that day, just a bunch of noise that would have been none of our business."

It is true that the city walls contain normalcy and many activities. The day that Jesus died would have been a normal day, in a normal city. The people would look much the same, only there would have been Roman soldiers wandering around instead of Israeli ones. The sun, the air, the smells, would be almost the same. I was struck by how ordinary the most holy city on the earth is. Jerusalem is ordinary people living surrounded by extraordinary history.

And then I think about how ordinary a day the day of the crucifixion would have been. I think the same about the day of resurrection. Ordinary day, ordinary time, while extraordinary things swirled around. Maybe that is how God works. It was an ordinary moment in time when the voice of God said, "Let there be light." It was an ordinary day when God spoke to Abraham. Now, we are just walking along an old city, and the ordinary turns extraordinary.

Extraordinary in the sense that this is just a city in a small country. People claim that holy things have happened here. Synagogues, churches and mosques are all over the place. People are proud of their heritage and their backgrounds. But, this is just a city among the countless cities of the world. It is not the holy sites that make it extraordinary. I think that it is the memory of what happened that makes it extraordinary. The Rev. Dr. Andrew Mayes has pointed out that the Holy Land seems to hinge on memory and hope. People remember extraordinary events and the hope for extraordinary things. In a sense they believe that God has acted here, and that God will act here again. How God and when God will do this is anyone's guess. Many people have made a career of predicting that action. How God acted is a matter of memory, and those memories move an extraordinary hope.

There is a story in the Gospel of Mark of a woman who wishes to touch Jesus to be healed. As he walked, and the crowd pressed in on him, she followed him. She was as ordinary as I am now. She and I do not share the same affliction, but she and I share affliction. In her time she reached for the healer. On the day I drank lemonade and watched people, I walked down and reached out to touch the Wailing Wall. I asked for healing too. It is just ordinary rock, hewn from regular quarries, set up to be a retaining wall for a temple area. The person who hewed it was just like me too. The person who designed the temple, just like me too. Ordinary people called into service, doing their own tasks, asking for their own healings, participating in the normal day of God.

What makes this city extraordinary is the ordinary people who allowed themselves to live their lives not seeking greatness or fame, but just lived their lives. They lived them amid the time they had, and these people lived their lives within the walls of this ordinary city where they found themselves living.

The themes that continue to rise up are memories, hope, boundaries and ordinary time. In our common life together we are swept up in a weird combination of all four. One does not need to come to Jerusalem to figure that out. The boundary of time keeps us in a set place. In a lifetime, we have only a few minutes really, and in those few minutes we get a sense of the divine in the ordinary lives we lead. We see it in the way we see ourselves reflected back in the people we love. We see it and we remember it and we lock it inside ourselves. With memory comes hope. My hope, my Christian hope, is in the name of the Lord. I say that a lot. Jesus took his cues from a memory, a memory of Exodus from bondage, from slavery. Hope for freedom from slavery, and a desire to be free from all bonds, even those that separate people from God becomes a theme of Jesus. God's desire to free each of us from the walls that surround us, to allow us a life that is free from boundary becomes a theme for Christians. So, even within the things that bind us, wall us in, within those we have a freedom that passes our understanding. We become ordinary people, bound in ordinary time, with ordinary feelings, but with an extraordinary freedom amid that living boundary.

Standing in front of the western wall, I imagine that touching the wall means touching the hope that lies beyond the wall, past the temple, past this living and into something else. Touching the wall means touching hope, an ordinary hope. Touching the wall means touching a memory— an ordinary memory of extraordinary things. In the end touching the wall means touching God. On the hill in Salem is a temple mount where people say many holy things occurred. When someone touches it he or she is aware of the ordinary souls who touched it before them.

In the old city I am only an ordinary person wandering around looking at ordinary things that cut through the thin places and for a moment were divine and instruments of

God. I become the keeper of that memory and that hope. I seek to touch and be healed in that memory and that hope. I share afflictions, boundaries, and time. In all of that I have a sense of wandering around as I find God.

III

Doors

There comes a point in a theological tourist's life that he stops trying to be profound and starts looking more like a humble, lost pilgrim. I had that day in Bethlehem. On that day I found myself sitting on the floor of the Church of the Nativity looking at that stone floor, and realizing that I was nothing more than a passerby. Any thoughts that I had on any subject from that time forward were simply silly reflections. Below the stones I was sitting on, St. Jerome lived for some thirty years in a cave translating the bible into Latin. Clergy from all ranks had filed through the small door into the cave below the altar to kneel and touch the rock that marks the place where Jesus was born. Countless tourists and pilgrims had made the trek into Bethlehem to the spot where I sat. Writing about this place is more like singing in a shower. Silly hymns that are out of tune. People passing by you are held captive by your songs.

My trip to the Church of the Nativity began with a trip outside of Jerusalem, to the Church of the Annunciation, which is reportedly the place where Elizabeth lived and where Mary traveled and stayed. It is a long walk up to the church. Once I walked to the gate I saw a sweeping view of the hill country. I found myself imagining Mary, young and newly pregnant, walking up to that place.

The next stop was the Church of John the Baptist, and the cave where he was reportedly born. I was more aware of the other tourists and their matching baseball hats than I was in awe of the birth of the proclaiming and baptizing one. I will need to revisit this place again and be more in awe.

After that we travelled into the West Bank, to Bethlehem and a place called the Shepherds Fields. After prayer and reflection in a traditional shepherd's cave, we were asked to spend fifteen minutes in silence. I wandered down into an old Byzantine monastary ruin. It was here that I began to take notice. From the edge of the monastary's ruins you get sense of the expanse of the countryside. I chose a bench near a small altar that was shaded by some pine trees and looked out onto the plain below. I imagined the shepherds having this same vantage point when suddenly up over the hill came the unearthly sight of angels. I thought about meeting angels. Nothing like that has ever happened to me. I hope it never does. Who would? In the bible, when angels show up normal life gets rearranged. I looked up through the pines, hoping to maintain my normalcy. From where I sat, the shade and the wind made it cool. The stark contrast between the sun and the shade was notable. Angels would show up anyway after we made our way to the Church of the Nativity.

As we walked onto the plaza of the famous church, I saw a procession. My first impulse was to film what I thought was a Church of the Nativity daily event, some local after lunch liturgical tradition, when I realized it was a funeral procession. The deceased was being carried along by a large group of men chanting hymns. I noticed that the funeral procession was being led by a cross. Then I noticed that the cross was followed by a young man carrying the top of the coffin. The coffin contained the body of an older man. There were no women in the procession.

After the funeral procession passed us, I saw the widow. She was very distraught and her family and friends were attending to her. The Church of the Nativity is not a museum. It is a living church. It is alive with people. It is more than the birthplace of Christ, it is the prayerful place of generations. It is a family church. It is a church that mourns as well as inspires. It is a place to celebrate birth and celebrate life and celebrate hope in death.

To get into the church I had to stoop. The first thing that struck me was, "Wow! This is the church of the Nativity! I am actually going into it." The second thought for me was, "What is the deal with all the hanging lights?" There were lights hanging down in a single line from the narthex through the nave and right up to the altar. The lights lead you to an altar area. From there, in order to see the cave, I stood in a line with my group and people from all over the world. On this day there were many people waiting to see the cave. A line of lights, a line of tourists, both lines marking the way to the birth of Jesus.

To get into the cave under the altar you take a series of steps down. At that point you are in front of a shrine. You are encouraged to kneel down and touch the stone. It is the same posture you take when opening the flue in a chimney. I had about three seconds in the shrine. I touched the stone, kissed the floor and stood back up again. I was then able to take a quick picture before I was asked to walk up and out on the other side. There were a few men who were sitting on a bench. I was jealous of them. I wanted to sit there for a few minutes more, maybe even get lost in the time, and wonder to myself what on earth all of this meant.

Outside of the cave we were taken into a second church, a Catholic church that is conjoined to the older Nativity church. Below this church is the cell of St. Jerome. I stood in his cell and wondered aloud what that symbol meant for me—a man spending thirty years of his life doing one thing, translating a bible.

As we left the Church of the Nativity, I took a picture of myself with the small door in the background. We loaded up on the bus and were driven home. The day was done.

I failed to mention one symbol that caught my attention earlier in the day. Bethlehem is in the West Bank and is under Palestinian control. To get there we had to go past a military checkpoint and drive through the newly erected wall. The wall is not a holy wall. It is stark, and the sense of division is fierce.

As we drove back to Jerusalem and to the college the thoughts swirled in my head, *small doors, walls, stones, shepherds, expanse, living, dying, traditions, annunciations, pregnant teens, hill country, pine trees, caves.*

I sit there on the bus and think—Mary must have been a woman of means. I have always pictured her as a peasant girl, but she must have come from a good family, a family with money. To get to her cousin Elizabeth's house she would have had to travel down from Nazareth, about a hundred miles. I have been around pregnant women before, and traveling a hundred miles anywhere, car or donkey, must have been uncomfortable. She would have had to spend the night in Jericho. Then she would have to make the rest of the journey to Elizabeth's house that would include a climb. She must have had attendants. So, she must have had money. I am not sure poor peasant girls could have journeyed to see their cousins as Mary is said to have done without some help. I wondered if this was her first time to visit, or if she had been there before and knew the way.

She might have even had to go. There is a part of me that wondered if she went to Elizabeth's to live until she was to deliver. Why risk the shame in your small hometown? Joseph probably picked her up on his way to Bethlehem for the census. It would seem strange for her to travel all the way back home to Nazareth and then just a month of two later travel all the way back to Bethlehem. A wealthier girl who was found pregnant and was sent to live with her cousin until her baby was due—or until the father of her child could come and get her—this was a new picture of Mary for me.

My thoughts turn to the Gospel's account that John and Jesus were second cousins, six months apart in age. After they were born, it is reported that Herod ordered all the boys under two to be murdered. Joseph takes his family to Egypt. Zechariah and Elizabeth hide John from Herod's murderers. The boys survive and go on to be famous each in his own way. Despite their fame, John ends up being beheaded by Herod, and Jesus crucified by Pilate.

I think further—we are taught, told, reminded that all of this is said to occur for the salvation of the world. For you and for me. The salvation of the check out girl with the nice smile and also the guy in the cubicle we cannot stand. These events happened so that the world might know that God is good. Really?

An unexpectedly pregnant teen? A massacre of other people's beloved children? A beheading? A crucifixion? And the salvation of the world has occurred?

There is a large wall that separates Bethlehem, the City of David from Jerusalem, the City of Peace. On the wall, there is a sign that read *Jerusalem and Bethlehem—Cities of Love*. I read that sign and think, "did Jesus die in vain?" Was Jesus resurrected for a wall? Did Mary carry a divine baby and birth it in a remote cave for barriers to be erected or to be torn down? Did Jerome translate a bible into a language all people could understand only to have everyone misunderstand the translation of "love your neighbor?" What sense does it make?

Then I think, "the door is small."

It struck me that the door is small. The man was carried away from his funeral. His funeral was a service of hope. His widow looked around for some sort of reassurance, comfort, and found it in the arms of her friends. The small door concentrates the light. When you open it, the light is very bright and shines directly on the path that you are to take to get into the church. The small door opens into an expansive place full of light. Lamps hang everywhere to shine light on the room.

The young girl knows. The baptizer knows. Jesus knows. Walls and politics come and go. Powerful people come and go. Rulers and commanders and dividers come and go. The little church on the hill has seen it. The stones where I sat have seen it. The little door opens. Our hearts open, just a little, and in that small space suddenly light shows the way. In my mind an uninvited angel sings in a whisper,

You are more than your politics.
You are more than your walls.
You are more than you realize.

The light shines in the darkness and the darkness does not overcome it. The door opens, the walls come down, we are new people. The angel sings some more,

You are a people of hope in the middle of
  separation and division.
You are a people who believe in bravery in the
  face of oppression.
You are a people who believe in the love of God
  for a creation.
You are a people who believe in the mystery of
  the witness of the shepherds.
You are a people who believe that in the middle
  of the pain the door will always open and the light will
  always shine inside.
You are a people who are willing to wait to kneel
  where wise men kneeled.
You are a people who are willing to say prayers for
  yourselves and the world.
You are a people who live.
  You are a people who die.
    You are a people who hope.

The angel sang and the small door shows the way. The salvation of the world did occur. Somehow we are deaf to the angels' voices. The pregnant teen, the massacre, the beheadings, the crucifixions still echo in our hearts, still make us desire something different for ourselves and our world. We do not want division, we do not want walls, we do not want war. The birth of something holy is announced in Bethlehem. From that announcement comes our hope. From those angels comes our memory. From that moment on we are changed and made new.

IV

The Sea of Galilee

This is Peter's house, and Jesus stayed there after healing Peter's mother. Here is the town where the little girl was brought back to life. There is the synagogue where he taught. That is a shoreline he walked. Over there is the land where he walked. This is a town where he wandered around. That is a mountain where he was transfigured. This is the sea he crossed. This is the sea where he swam. This is sea he calmed.

And now you are here...

I grew up going to church. It is what we did. In the fourth grade I won a scholarship for perfect attendance in Sunday School. I had perfect attendance, but I was by no means perfect. Mrs. Coleman was a good teacher and put up with me each week. When I went to seminary she sent me a note that said she had always hoped that someday one of her Sunday School students would end up a priest. She expressed her pride in her work as a Sunday School teacher. She was proud of her students.

Growing up in the church, going to Sunday School, I heard the biblical stories in very simple ways. I colored Jesus and the disciples in with a crayon. I built a wall of Jericho with macaroni and kernels of corn. I made a bible village with milk cartons, Popsicle sticks, sawdust, and glue. Later in seminary I re-visited those same stories. I learned how to think critically about the texts. I learned to listen to the texts of our faith tell an academic story.

Over a weekend I went to the place the texts describe. I was forever changed.

I do not think you can come to this part of the world for the first time and not be a little bit overwhelmed by the Sea of Galilee. At the important sites you are a theological tourist. You stand in line waiting for the holy ride. You get on the ride and then you get off the ride and that is done. The first few days felt as if I was in some archeological Epcot Center with a milieu of religious sound and food. It was the Sea of Galilee that centered me.

My first glimpse of the sea was on the approach from Nazareth. The sea sits 209 meters below sea level. We drove down to it. It is not very large. From almost any vantage point I could see the whole thing. Our accommodations were on the shore. After I found my room I walked down to the water. I then lost all sense of time. From milk carton villages to the actual location, a thirty-year pilgrimage, from Sunday School to the moment my feet touched the water. I was standing along a shoreline where Jesus of Nazareth stood. Where Peter, James and John stood. Where Andrew stood. Where Mary stood. Where five thousand stood. Where countless pilgrims have stood. Here I was, some kid from the United States, from Texas, looking over at the opposite side. I thought about the crazed man in chains from the story in Mark. I thought about the pigs full of a legion of demons that went running wild into the water after they were exorcised from the man in chains. I thought about the boat full of disicples in the storm. I thought about the walking on the water. I thought about the Sermon on the Mount. I was overcome with the history of Christianity in the places in and around Galilee. We have been telling our children the stories that occurred here for two thousand years. And in some way, the place hadn't changed too much.

The shoreline has risen and receded. Houses have been abandoned and rebuilt. Countless lives have come and gone, but the landscape itself has remained pretty steady. As I scanned the shoreline from a boat, as I swam in the water, as I drove over to Mt. Tabor, as I sat in Capernaum—everywhere I went in Galilee—I got a sense of place, of definition, of perspective. I had spent so many years conjuring up in my mind what it all looked like. I spent time coloring within the lines, choosing the colors just so to make the village look just right. I had made up my mind based on pictures and the words of others. And, finally, I was looking at the Sea of Galilee. It became the most important site for me at that point on my pilgrimage.

Before we made it to Nazareth and the Sea of Galilee, we visited Caesarea Maritima, a ruin on the Mediterranean Sea. King Herod had a palace there. There was once an important port there. Aqueducts running from Mt. Carmel supplied the water. Crusaders built a fort. It had a theater, a hippodrome, amazing mosaics. It was once vibrant. After history, wars, politics, and the sea all that is left is a hint of its vibrancy. I had to picture its glory in my mind. When I stood in Herod's palace I could see him swimming in his sea-fed pool, getting out and being handed a towel. King Herod: with all his power, not much that he built has lasted. The sound of the sea reminds me that the things we construct waste away with the roll of the tide.

As I move from the Mediterranean Sea to the sea of Galilee, I compare Herod's palace by the sea with the Church of the Primacy of St. Peter. Not the church itself, but the people who come there. It is on the Sea of Galilee, right along the shore. I sat with my group and celebrated the Eucharist in a small outdoor chapel. Next to us was a group of Italians doing the same. Down the way a group of young people from France was doing likewise. Up and down the property believers were enacting a famous meal together. We were singing, we were praying, we were listening to scripture, we were asking forgiveness, we were passing the peace. We were breaking bread, sharing wine. That rhythm is as familiar to me as the tide. Only this kind of tide does not wear me away. This builds me up. As we sat there listening to all of these languages celebrate this holy act, it was Pentecost all over again. Everyone in his or her own language understood the spirit of God. We got it. We did not need anything other than the shade of a tree and the tempo of the Eucharist to understand the message of the Gospels. And there we were, two thousand years later; we were living stones, living palaces, living aqueducts, living hippodromes, living churches.

There must be something to our proclamation. We must have some truth inside our words. There must be something else happening inside the hearts of so many. Surely after two millennia things would have calmed down more. Surely after so many years of textual study and form criticism and theological barnstorming we would have found the trick played on us. So there must be something to our story that each generation finds compelling. Otherwise the only thing you would have heard at the shore of the Sea of Galilee that day would have been the lapping of the water against a ruin. Instead all I heard on that day was the sound of the faithful voices, speaking and singing in many languages, each of them joining together making one statement of faith.

Later on in the day we stopped by Yardenit, a site on the Jordan river reserved for believers to be baptized or renew their baptismal vows. I swam with my pants on. By the end of the day it was hot, and new friend dared me and I did it. Not the most religious of experiences, but it did cool me off. I found myself floating next to some people in white robes. It was an odd sight. There in the river were people from all over, in the water for one reason or another. Some to escape the heat, others to be faithful. I guess I was both.

As the weekend ended, and we headed back to Jerusalem, we went to Mt. Tabor. This is the site of the Church of the Transfiguration. I stood upon that high place and felt the cool air and left prayers for my friends in the church nave. From there I could see the old road to Jerusalem. Our guide pointed out that this was a fulcrum place in the Gospel story. Galilee was the backdrop and played an important role in the ministry of Jesus. I could see Galilee from the mountain. Jerusalem had its own role to play. I got a sense of the passage in Luke 9.51, "and he set his face to go to Jerusalem." The transfiguration leads him to another ministry, to the city. The sea and the city. These two places are the environments for stories that change people's lives.

From there we drove south and we passed through two military checkpoints to get into Jericho. Jericho is on the West Bank, a Palestinian territory. Jericho is the rest stop before you make your way to Jerusalem. I remembered my thoughts about Jesus' mother stopping here on her way to see Elizabeth. Jesus had probably stopped here with his family as they made their way back from Egypt to Nazareth. We stopped there for lunch and a look at the famous Walls of Jericho.

We drove through the Judean Desert. We stopped and climbed up onto an overlook and found a panoramic view the desert. Up there we could see from Jericho to the Mount of Olives. Below us was the old Roman road linking Jerusalem with Jericho. As the wind blew there was a stark contrast to the land of Galilee. The desert's color was broken by a blue horizon. I looked down and could see some trees near the wadi. I looked out and saw one lone tree. That was the tree I imagined Jesus sitting under resting as he made his way from Galilee to Jerusalem.

In my mind, I see him propped up against that tree, and thirsty. I see his mind being lost to the wind and the heat. I see him hungry. I hear the devil in his ears. I see him wishing things might be otherwise. I see him wishing for the Galilee again. Cool water, green fields, family and friends. I see him thinking about the powers of the day, Romans, King Herod, the Temple clergy. I see him thinking about the people he has healed. I see him there under that tree wondering aloud to no one in particular, "what am I supposed to do?" After no answer in particular, I see him get up and keep going on.

I see him in this desert. He is walking up the old Roman road to Jerusalem. There he goes, this one guy, followed by a band of men and women, walking up a hill into the city. He will send someone ahead to borrow a colt. In a few hours he will mock the powers that hold sway over the day. In a few days he will disrupt the balance of power in the Temple. In a week he will change the world.

He didn't build one palace, and he didn't conquer one city. In fact he ends up dead. There is a mystery here. How did one dead man from Galilee trump the power and the prestige of the Roman Empire and King Herod? Here is the mystery of my faith. Two thousand years later, people from many places, or many languages come and see this power conversion. Baptism and Eucharist make holy fortifications out of living stones. Each generation makes a new palace, a new temple, for the holy to reside. The world's scales were tipped by Jesus. His descision to walk into Jerusalem would transform the world. His death would make life.

V

Siege

In the year 70 CE the Romans destroyed the Temple in Jerusalem. Their ferocity is compelling. The Jewish revolts had made them very angry. To send a clear message to the Jewish people the Romans ripped the Temple off the face of the earth. All that remains are the basic building blocks of a once great and impressive work of praise and devotion to God. By destroying the Temple, the Romans in effect tore the heart out of the people. It sent the people scattering. It is hard to understand the use of force to destroy the house of worship of someone else. It brings to mind the burning of churches in the recent history of the United States. Our houses of worship are consecrated spaces where the divine can mingle with creation. We call them houses of God. Destroy one and you are destroying something more than an ornate building. When we violently destroy the places of prayer of another we not only injure the person, we in some way injure God. I do not understand the rage and hate that must be present for someone to choose this action. The Romans were that mad. The Romans were that powerful.

When you stand next to the wall of the Temple today you marvel at how the people of antiquity managed to quarry and build with such massive stones. When you see the pile of stones the Romans threw down, you marvel at their rage. Standing there you see the most creative and innovative part of our human character, and you see the most hideous and destructive part of our human character.

The narrative of the ministry of Jesus is set with the Roman Empire as its backdrop. The early Christian church grew up amid the turmoil and confusion after the Romans destroyed Jerusalem. Within the confusion, the early church showed how creative and healing God can be in the stories of Jesus and his healing and feeding ministry. I am interested that in its history the church went from showing creativity to showing a more destructive side in its inquisitions and crusades. We seem to have two poles of human character, two extreme possibilities. We live most of our lives in the middle. Most of us are neither too creative nor too destructive. We are average. We are normal. We sometimes register on the high end of the middle, raging at people or having flashes of creative genius. But most of us, I have found, are regular. It is the regular people that I find more interesting in Jerusalem. It is those regular people who were caught up in the Roman massacre that I mourn. It is those regular people whom Jesus fed and healed. I am one of them, sometimes filled with rage, sometimes filled with creativity, but mostly regular and in need of healing.

Down from the Temple Mount are the ruins of the pools of Bethesda. They sit next to St. Anne's church. It is there that people would come to bathe in the pools in order to be healed of their illness and infirmities. There is a scene in John's gospel where Jesus goes to the pool and finds a man who has been ill for thirty-eight years. The man has trouble getting to the pool. Jesus tells the man to "Rise up, take your mat and walk." (John 5.2-9). It is a powerful scene. People read it as if Jesus commanded the man in a loud voice. I read it differently. I think Jesus says it quietly, close to the man's ear.

When I visited this place I tried to get a sense of the scene that Jesus would have encountered. There must have been so many ill and infirm waiting around for a chance to get into the pools. The city of Austin, Texas has a community pool called Barton Springs. It is the only reference I can draw on to compare the two places. Both places are jammed with bathers, only at Bethseda, the bathers are sick. As Jesus and his companions walk into the pool area they are amazed at what they see. Maybe they have only heard stories of this healing place and had come to see for themselves. Whatever the reason they were there, as I stand there I imagine that Jesus looks at all of the ill and the infirm and chooses this one man. I do not know why, but he did. To see that many sick people would be overwhelming. Looking around Jesus sees this one man. This one man has no one to help him get into and out of the water. It would seem the other ill and infirm had people to help them. For thirty-eight years no one had bothered to help this man. Suddenly we have Jesus looking at him, then glancing back at the other sick people, turning looking back to this man, giving a look at his disciples, and then kneeling next to man. Quietly he says to him, "Do you want to be healed?" After the man responds "yes," Jesus speaks again in an even more quiet voice; it is almost like a secret between this one man and this one healer. Nothing showy, so as not to attract attention, Jesus commands the man, "rise up, take your mat and walk." And the man does.

After thirty-eight years he is gone from the pools. I see the others taking no notice. He had become like a part of the furniture; it would be a few days later that people would wonder where he went. I imagine someone figured he had died. But he had not died. He was restored to normalcy, to being regular. I wonder what he did. I wonder what that man, after almost four decades of being locked in his bodily prison, did. After having a stranger walk up to me and heal me, I am curious what I would do.

Well I know.

While I was sitting by the remains of the pool I asked a priest colleague from New Zealand, a person I hardly knew, I asked her to pray for me. She obliged. Setting her hands on my head she prayed. I usually do the praying; it is rare for people to pray over me. As she began, her hands anointed my head with oil. Then she did something more, she anointed my hands as well. She asked for God's blessing on me and my family and allowed the Holy Spirit to do the rest. Sitting near a wall on the grounds where Jesus healed that one man, I felt healed as well. I am not sure of what affliction I was healed, but I believe I was healed of my own self-importance and my own self-doubt. I was made regular again. I am not exactly sure what to do with myself. Who cares? The point for me is that I am made whole to live the life of a normal human being. I may do great things, and for that matter I may do awful things, but the reality that I am normal and have reclaimed the witness of normalcy unlocks the future for me. Romans may slaughter me tomorrow. Today I am okay, and normal and restored.

I think that man that Jesus healed did the same. Who cares what he did; he got up and walked back into being a human again. No longer stuck, he was freed. I imagine his freedom allowed him to walk down the road and through the city gate and up to the top of the Mount of Olives to get a better view of the city. Where he went from there is anybody's guess. The same goes for me, and for all who feel they have been healed by God, it doesn't matter where we go. It is the freedom to walk again into a life that can now be fully lived: that is the point. I am normal again. In my normalcy I feel the grandeur of God in my soul. I am his child and he is my God. From there it flows into how I am as a husband and father and a priest. From there it pours into how I am as a friend and a colleague. From there it continues on into an interaction with the creation that is seen with fresh eyes.

The Romans came in a fit of anger and destroyed all that they could destroy. The same is true for each of us. In our lives the Romans come and lay siege to us. They look like cancer, or addiction, or mental illness, or divorce, or financial ruin, or sick children, or dying parents, or states of war, random violence, or encounters with the extreme evil of the human condition. The Romans come for the normal people too. Sometimes you cannot run away. Sometimes the siege takes our life. Sometimes all we can do is cry.

However, in the event these extremes do come, they are not met with fear. They are met with courage, with dignity, with normal human life. The power of a siege is fleeting, but human healing is forever. The healing I am writing of is one that allows us an internal freedom, an internal strength. The external parts no longer matter. Walking away with our mat, we seek to find others who desire to be healed. We find others who cannot make it down to the pool alone; others who are not aware of how normal they are, how wonderfully normal they are as created beings. We are to find them in the middle of the siege and show them how to escape through the walls that encircle them and lead them away from the war. This is the work of the priesthood of all believers.

When we do this, we lean towards our greater nature, toward the other side of the Roman siege and into the construction of a new Temple for God. When we take our own healed souls and combine them with other healed souls, we become a living temple, stronger than any army and more holy than any site on earth. Our church is one of flesh and blood, bone and skin, mind and soul. Our church is not one that can be destroyed by blowing up a building or burning down a house of worship. God is only in the church when we are together as a people of God. Burn us down and we rise back up. It is the message of the Gospels. The Romans won Jerusalem on that day in

70 CE, but they didn't crush the Temple. No one can kill the Spirit of God. It is that spirit that Jesus has and it is that spirit that we share. God heals us, makes us whole, and nothing can change our normal life. Nothing. Not even death.

VI

Pawn Shops

You have two choices to get to the top of Masada. You can climb the Snake Path, which is a trail that leads up to the top, or you can take a cable car. I took the cable car.

At the top, you suddenly understand why the first people to ascend came here. You understand why Herod chose this site. The views are amazing. You can see a complete panorama of the desert and the Dead Sea. The air is dry and you can feel the northern breeze. The ruins there give you a sense of someone's country home with all of the amenities of city life. Herod had baths and porticos and storage buildings. He built a three-level living space on the cliffs of the northern face. The water system is ingenious. The area is known for its flash floods. There were two channels that ran down the western side. When the floods came, the water ran down the channels and then collected into cisterns about half way up the mountain. The water was then hauled up to larger storage cisterns on top. A modern person stops in the heat and wonders out loud, "How on earth they do all of this without a cell phone, the internet, and a copying machine I will never know." It is true, the place is amazing. Herod was known for his buildings. While Masada is a marvel, I kept thinking it is also a graveyard.

Masada is venerated by the Jewish people much like the Alamo is by Texans. Both places are known for acts of heroism in the face of overwhelming foes. Like the Alamo, Masada is a place where people come to remember that heroism. Just as the Alamo is revered as a treasure of the people of Texas, Masada is revered as a national treasure of Israel, and rightfully so. However, the tragedy that occurred on Masada lends itself to remind us that like the Alamo, Masada is also a graveyard. Both places were built for one purpose, and then through a series of tragic events, came to symbolize something completely other. The Alamo was a mission church. Masada became a palace and later a refuge. Both are now touchstones reminding their respective descendants of sacrifice and endurance and dying.

Graveyards have the same function. The headstones and markers remind us of our ancestors and the fate that waits for each of us. Be it the Mexican Army, the Roman Army, or just plain living, we are surrounded by existence and we will not get out alive. The courage to live with that knowledge is, in my opinion, freeing.

After Herod, and when the Romans came to sack Jerusalem, a group of people, around nine hundred or so, barricaded themselves on Masada. There, they hoped to defend against and maybe even survive the Romans who had come to kill them. The Masada scene is really interesting to me. The Romans had just wiped out all of Jerusalem. Why waste their time on this bunch? The Romans surrounded the area with a rock wall fortification, built encampments at strategic points to insure no one could get in or out. They then began to build a rampart, the remains of which still reach the western side. All of that energy and all of those soldiers used to capture a very small group of people. All of this done in a desert in conditions very unsuitable for human beings. They surrounded Masada. The Romans encamped and laid siege. Working hard to smash the small group of Jewish people.

They finally succeeded in breaching the wall. For some reason they waited a day to take the fortress. When they got inside, ready for a fight, they found that everyone was dead. A mass suicide had taken place. These last survivors had chosen a self-death over a torture-death. These men and women had chosen to take their own lives rather than be subjected to lives as slaves. In doing so, they had snatched a victory away from their tormenters.

There is an odd quiet there. I imagine it sounds like the day the Romans entered the walls. You wander around in the heat looking for shade and finding none. The views are breathtaking, but so is the silence. You are aware that you are in a place of dying. Tragedy is there. The memory of that tragedy still resonates. Metaphors for the living rise up out of that tragedy. In some strange way, hope emerges. Each generation looks on the tragedy of the past and hopes for the future. Masada did that for me. The Israeli army takes an oath on Masada. The soldiers say, "Masada shall not fall again." There is pride in the sacrifice of so many. There is hope that their sacrifice will not need to happen again. There is strong national pride in that statement. In the quiet you can hear the soldiers saying it under their breath, an oath that they will defend their country with their lives. Confidence and courage in the face of possible destruction. Hope that this tragedy will not need to happen again.

North of Masada are the ruins of a small religious community called Qumran. The ruins show the remains of a devoted life lived in the desert. What makes Qumran intriguing is the discovery of the ancient manuscripts the community used. Those pieces of writing, called the Dead Sea Scolls, have changed biblical scholarship as we knew it. Some see threads of Qumran thought in the words of John the Baptist and even Jesus. The community may be one that John the Baptist knew, and that maybe even Jesus knew. From Qumran you are not far from where the Jordan enters the Dead Sea. People say it is there that Jesus was baptized by John, which adds to the legend. Qumran is mysterious, and its treasures are priceless. Being there, I felt a connection in time to my own faith. Somehow these people made a life in the desert, and their thoughts echoed into the faith life I now share.

Masada and Qumran are two sites of powerful memory. They each speak of the fleeting time in the existence for human beings. They also speak of the power of the human being. At these two sites we are able to see ourselves in our most creative and most devout. We are able to see ourselves in our most vulnerable and our most resilient.

We are creative people. We do creative things. We use the tools our generations give us and we make amazing things. We are also devout. We have within us the ability to transcend our *selves* and look reflectively at something outside of that *self*. I call this God. I find that there is something more to me, something outside of me that is active and alive. I am limited in my speech and my ability to articulate my existence. For me, this transcendence is like moving through layers of atmosphere, getting finally outside of the earth and into the layer of space. There are no more words, it is just space. Likewise, devotion moves me through the layers of my living, the noise of the everyday, the quiet of a sanctuary, the stillness of my mind and then finally to a place that is called God. God is more than me. Which seems simple, but in my own hubris I forget that fact. And even though living often feels like a no-win situation, a life surrounded by Romans on every side. And even though my destruction is imminent, there is still that sense that there is something more. This thing, this sense of "more" this is what I call God.

Back in the tour bus after visiting these sites, from one window I watched the light bounce off of the Dead Sea. From the other I looked up at the desert hillsides. As we drove along I thought to myself that I am more than a forgotten gravestone. I am alive in the lives that I meet and live with and relate. I am alive in the lives I helped make. As a human being I share a mystery, and I need to remember my devotionals. Not so much devotional prayers, but those devotional moments where I look at another human being and see the face of God. All anybody needs to do is look into the eyes of the living and for a brief moment set aside our initial reactions and see their eyes. It is there you see the mirror of God.

Romans will surround us. Living will rob us. Death will come for us. That is a truth we cannot escape. Suicide might look like the better measure. Despair is real. Yet, I hope for something more than these in the face of certain tragedy. I hope for God.

As I rode along, for some strange reason I found myself hearing a John Prine song in my head: "Souvenirs" where he sings,

> *I hate graveyards and old pawn shops*
> *for they always bring me tears,*
> *can't believe the way they rob me*
> *of my sweet heart souvenirs*

I agree. Graveyards remind me of the fleeting time, and how I will be robbed one day, I just will. Yet I stand differently in my living through my devotion to God. I will be robbed of my souvenirs, all of those things will be pawned off. Someone, or something will take them from me, sell them away. Nothing will be left, except the graveyard my body will lie in and the pawnshop that sells my memories. What does remain is a mystery. What does remain, that echoes out, is the love that I have made and the love that I see all around me. My family and my friends are more than collectible souvenirs, they are a chain of living beings that interlock me to the holy. That is mysterious to me. How is this possible? How am I connected to someone even after the grave? How is it possible to stand in tragedy and imagine hope? It is a mysterious part of our living, and an aspect of our selves that is true.

Living is more than waiting for the Romans to come for us. In the middle of their siege the people at Masada built a synagogue. A place of prayer. I am encouraged to do the same. In the middle of my living I carve out a space for prayer. I may be surrounded, and death may be coming, but I can still pray. I can still be devout. I can still be faithful. I can still be God's own while I have breath in my lungs and beyond. Carving out a place of prayer in the middle of living is how I manage to stay alive and avoid the temptations to see life as futile and unlivable. I am not a Masada, nor am I a Qumran. Those are ruins and lost. What is there, what echoes from there, what I am as well, is a life among many lives, and that living self allows me a great gift. The gift I will eternally have as my eyes close on my last day is the love I shared while I was on the journey. That gift comes from God.

That gift cannot be pawned.

It is mine forever.

VII

Justina

Reality is a funny word. When I was in college I took a metaphysics class and we got into the typical conversation about what is really "real" in the world. How do you know? Quantum physics has pushed on that a little more. I heard a lecture once on quantum physics and the lecturer used the example of a cloud. What exactly is the cloud? The shape you look at? Well it just changed. The color of it? That shifts with the light and the air. Is a cloud its molecules? Is the cloud its ice crystals? We know what makes a cloud. We know that clouds form and change and form again. When you point at a cloud you cannot say exactly what you are pointing at even though it is right in front of you and you are aware that you are seeing it. A cloud is real, but its reality shifts with every second of its formation. The universe is the same way. The reality of it just changed as I wrote these words.

I went to many sites in my short time in Jerusalem. I was told that many of the spots I saw were the actual sites of a particular event. I was told the story of the site, and many of the stories I have heard before. Each site I visited made me realize that history and memory are funny things. There seems to be a need for tangible places, spots marked for history and pilgrims, places that make logical sense to the passerby.

Near the end of my time in Jerusalem, I visited the Syrian Orthodox church of St. Mark. It is the reported site of the upper room where the disciples gathered with Jesus on the night before his passion. The upper room is the site of the institution of the Eucharist. The upper room is the site of the foot washing. The upper room is the site of the first appearances of Jesus after his resurrection. At St. Mark's, to get to the upper room, you go down.

The upper room is now the lower room, below the church. It was explained to me that over time, the topography of the city caught up with upper room then surpassed it. It was "upper" at one time, but now it is down.

I met Justina there. She is a woman who left her life as a mathematics teacher to come and care for the church. She is proud of her faith and its historical place in

Christianity. She has settled in Jerusalem to guard her faith. Justina takes her role in the Christian story very seriously. She loves God and it shows. Listening to her sing the Lord's Prayer is oddly mesmerizing. Her quixotic passion for her faith made me want to have more passion for my own.

As we sat in the church, Justina told the story of the upper room. She spoke of the house and the meal that was prepared there. She spoke of the signal the disciples were looking for to find the house, a man carrying a jar of water. Justina pointed out that only women carried water in jars, which is why the signal was out of context and easy to spot in a busy city that was being prepared for Passover. She said that man was St. Mark. She spoke of the last supper itself, Judas' betrayal, Jesus' bread and wine. She spoke of two recent encounters with the divine. One was an appearance of Jesus to a French woman three months prior, and another was the gift of tongues to a Russian policeman who spoke only Russian and Hebrew who was in a conversation with Justina who speaks only Aramaic and English. She spoke of the upper room and the appearance of Jesus to the disciples after his resurrection.

Apart from the cross and the tomb, the accounts in the upper room are the most important to the story. It was here at St. Mark's that these events took place. Maybe.

Our group left there and went to the other traditional site of the upper room. A room that is really "upper." It is called the Cenacle and it is on Mount Zion. Walking into it, I noticed something was missing. This upper room had no Justina. We were told the story of that space, but it seemed more of a passageway than a room. It had been a chapel, a mosque, and it had been important to the Crusaders, but it was missing a person to tell its story. My mind turned back to Justina and her church of St. Mark.

I may be duped, but I do not care. Who cares if the lower room at St. Mark's may not be the upper room of the bible. For a minute I suspended my disbelief and cynicism and allowed Justina's passion for her Lord and her space to be the truth. As I sat in that church of St. Mark's I was overcome with a sense of mission in my faith. I could see the disicples in that space eating a meal. I could picture Judas leaving the room. I felt the moment when those disciples were huddled together in the upper space with the doors locked. I sensed the anxiety of the post crucifixion. And, I could see the resolve of the disciples after the resurrection appearances. This was the upper room for me. I found a renewed sense of mission there. I found the Holy Spirit at the Syrian Orthodox church of St. Mark the Evangelist.

Mission and Holy Spirit are Christian buzzwords. For me they are white noise in Christian language. Every church has a mission statement, including my own. Every church claims to be guided by the Holy Spirit, including my own. We say these words glibly. Sometimes we say them arrogantly. Many times we say them like we mean them, but really we do not know what we are saying at all. Too much of the time we have a mission as a church, but it is to ourselves. All too often we say we are filled with the power of the Holy Spirit but it is for ourselves and those close to us. We do not really understand what we are saying; we mimic what we were taught to say and we have become used to saying it over time. We see others getting the Holy Spirit each week in their churches. We see others who seem to be filled with a sense of mission for their faith. Maybe they are. I would wager that the majority of us have not one clue what it means. I certainly did not. I do now, but up until the moment I met Justina and sat in her church I realized I did not.

I am convinced that if someone has a sure sense of Christian mission, if he or she is full of the Holy Spirit, then they will live the rest of their life without fear. For too long I have lived in *some odd fear of some future possibility of what maybe might happen if certain scenarios occurred.* I have lived my life afraid that I could lose my wife, my children, my money, my job, my life. I have lived my life in a worry about the opinions of other people. I have spent much of my time in an external way, wasting valuable living time on fear and worry and doubt. To see Justina's lower-upper room changed that for me. If those disciples could get up and walk out of there and change the world, then I could change the world too. I would get up and walk out of my fear and worry and doubt. God calls us and we should go. The first disciples did. So did those who were first to receive the message of hope: they went. Each generation since then has walked without fear but with encouragement from the Holy Spirit. All the way to Justina to me and to you, we have seen it, that courage in the face of living. We have a mission to proclaim in word and deed all the things we believe about our Christian faith and heritage. The call to proclaim is not the noise of buzzwords and slogans, it is the language of the heart and soul.

A short walk down from the Cenacle, you exit the gates of the old city and walk to the church of Galicantu, the church of St. Peter, and the traditional home of the High Priest, Caiaphas. Here is told the story of Peter's denial. Archeologists have found underground cisterns that may have been used as jail cells. Recently they have uncovered an ancient flight of stone stairs that lead down into the valley toward the Mount of Olives.

From this church I could trace with my eyes Jesus' movements from the upper room, to the Garden of Gethsemane, up the steps to Caiaphas' house, down into the holding cells, then back out again and to the city and Pilate. I stand in the silence of this place and among the ruins of buildings and get a feel for a courtyard and the tragedy of Peter's denial. Like the upper room, I have no way of knowing for sure if this is the actual site. When you visit you can be the judge of these sites. However, while I was standing there, mission and the Holy Spirit once again entered my thoughts. It was the stone stairs that captured my imagination.

The events that surround the birth of our Christian life are dramatic. I cannot keep my mind from the notion of walking. Walking into something that will kill you. Walking out of an upper room to proclaim a message of hope and resurrection. Walking out into the world of Asia Minor to tell strangers of the hope found in the message of Jesus of Nazareth. Walking out of one way of living into another. Walking down a flight of stairs to look up. Walking up a flight of stairs to care for a crying child. Walking in a life of courage instead of a life of fear. Walking with a sense of mission to proclaim a message of salvation. Walking amid the reality of persecution. There I stood at the foot of those ancient stairs seeing Jesus walking down to Pilate, and Peter walking up to deny Jesus, and the whole of human history about to change its steps and in doing so, changing the life of all of us, even me.

As Jesus walked down those stairs, with each step the ingathering of the world began. With each step the whole world was being changed. We all see ourselves at one moment in our faith life as Peter, denying Jesus at the top of the stairs. We need to remember that with each step down towards Jerusalem, Jesus was gathering the doubts and preparing to shatter them. They have been shattered. The reality we have now is not fading as if it were a cloud in quantum flux. The reality we have in the Christian message is the stirring of our hearts and the call of our mission as people of faith. A mission that has us singing the Lord's Prayer with Justina every step of the way.

VIII

Graves

The Mount of Olives is situated directly across the Kidron Valley from the Temple Mount. On the slope of this area is the Garden of Gethsemane. It is here in the Gospel stories that Jesus has his last freedom before being arrested and crucified. The area is terraced in such a way that you get a good sense of the quote, "Sit here while I pray." (MK 14.32). You can see Jesus move to a higher point, leaving the rest of his disciples below. You are able to get some privacy while still being in sight of the others. At a crest of the hill, you can turn and look back at the city across the valley. You get a good look at the Temple Mount. It was odd for me to be there, in the quiet of a small church built in the shape of a teardrop.

It is odd because I am retracing someone else's journey, someone else's pain. This retracing has set me in a place of impending doom. Here a man struggled with himself to follow the path he had found himself wandering. I am beginning to think that Jesus was sure he was supposed to heal and feed people. I am beginning to understand that he was aware of himself in that work. I feel that he knew what he was doing in his protests against the Temple moneychangers and his conflicts with the religious authorities. But then he might have thought it had gone too far. Being betrayed and arrested will send him into unknown territory. Sure, he spoke of his demise, "The Son of Man must be betrayed and handed over to them..."(MK 10.32) But now it is here. Maybe there could be another way? Maybe this ministry could continue on without this dying part. Think of all of the healing that could be done. Think of the lives that could be changed if this part were not to be played out. What will happen to these disciples? What will happen to his family? The good work they had started has taken hold. Change might occur. Change might occur without this next part.

They say that while he prayed his nerves shook him, almost splitting him in two as his sweat was like blood. After an unknown amount of time in prayer, we read of his resolve. There comes a moment of peace in an absolute handing over of self to the void of living. He will let the chips fall and say to the empty air:

Your will be done, not mine.
After all I am your creation, and
all that I have done and taught came from you.
Your will be done, not mine.

There on a hillside opposite a temple made of stone, Jesus stepped out of the living freedom we hold dear and offered his *self* to be arrested into the unknown future of living.

Apart from my grandmother, I have yet to lose anyone I hold dear. I dread that day. I have walked that loss with other people close to me, my parishioners and friends, but I have never suffered that pain myself. Obviously I will someday. It is a matter of time really. Like anybody, I am not looking forward to that time.

As you walk toward the bottom of the Mount of Olives you pass graveyard upon graveyard. As you look across at the city of Jerusalem, you are aware that you are surrounded by thousands of graves on each side of the valley. I could not help but think about dying as I walked down this narrow road on a steep incline. I thought about Jesus' death; I thought about my own. Then my thoughts turned to three particular deaths I experienced early on in my life as a priest.

In the first year of my ordained ministry I walked with three families as three of their loved ones, three women, died. One was five, one was seventeen and one was thirty-six. It was an intense time for me as a priest. Each death was tragic. One was a young girl, one a young woman, and one a young wife and a mother of two. I watched three sets of families grieve in very profound ways. I am still touched by those experiences. I have many times wondered how to articulate these events and their effect on me as a person and as a priest. As I walked down the road toward the Garden of Gethsemane, passing by these graveyards, surrounded by them, a phrase came to me, "women of the resurrection." These three now know something I do not know. They understand a mystery that I do not understand but peculiarly enough I proclaim. In their dying they are part of what is called the "cloud of witnesses." These three people mark the reality and the hope. They each represent a distinct aspect of Christianity to me: The Child, The Adolescent, and The Adult. These three aspects of the Christian life are on display in the stories that unfolded there in the Kidron valley as Jesus moves across the valley to his trial and crucifixion. They are also on display in our own lives as we live out the life given to us. They are on display as we also say, "Your will be done."

The first one is the female child full of potential. She has the privilege of being able to play and be free. She is not fettered by objectivity or undone by the pull of social convention. She can be a tomboy if she wants to be a tomboy. She can play with dolls if she wants to play with dolls. She has the freedom to think and wonder as *Sophia* or wisdom. She has the freedom to laugh like Eve as a new female creation. She is at once content with herself and her dreams, and all is new. Her eyes reveal all that is possible in the world. When she dies among us, a part of the very fabric of our human nature dies with her. When we lose her, we feel the pain Eve felt when she left the garden. Losing her is to suffer the pain of expulsion from the presence of God. All was good. Then all is bad.

The second is the adolescent. Tragically aware of the truth. The world sets her into boxes and sets her into categories and insists she not be what and who she is, a life-giver. She is trying to claim a moment of her life for herself, but no one understands her. She wants to dance and no one will let her. They allow the boys to have the power. But a boy's participation in the equation is limited. Boys only deliver one part of the creative force of life. Women carry the life inside them. The adolescent sees herself torn between two worlds, heaven and earth. She is able to carry life like God, but she has to endure living like a human. When she dies among us, the hope and the potential of all of us die with her.

The third is the life-giver adult. She is the mother who has participated in the creation. Mary. *Theotokos*. God Bearer. Men do not understand her. I certainly do not understand. To think about her is to try and understand what God is up to. What God is up to is making life. Making a life appear seemingly out of nowhere, out of a void, through her. After life is made, she is called to keeping life safe and keeping life healthy. Her duty is to an organic life, a retelling of the sixth day of creation. The potential each time a child is born. When the mother dies among us, creation is lost and our tears are not for her only, but for the lost children she might have carried and those she will no longer nurture.

In the garden of Gethsemane Jesus has all three aspects of these women of the resurrection crashing down on him. The child, the adolescent, the adult, these are all there with him as he prays. It is all lost soon. He will lose the child, lose the adolescent, lose the adult, these parts of his *self* as the world is about to demand its unworthy due. He will lose his freedom as he is placed in a role he may not want to play. He will have his children, his disciples, taken from him and his body will be left to die. Jesus will not be able to see Galilee again. Jesus will no longer be able to speak of his hopes. Jesus will be ending his creative human ministry. For the last time he will be free, soon humanity will chain him. Soon his body will not be his own. Soon all, from a human perspective, all will be uncertain.

As I walked across the street and into Jerusalem I thought about those three women, and their three natures, and the loss of those natures in the world. I thought about their families and the tears and hurt. I thought about the small coffin and the tiny life that was gone. I thought about the rain falling on my prayer book as we lowered a teenager into the ground. I thought about that mother, whose last words to me were, "it is not fair." I thought about Judas and the arresting body. I thought about Jesus being led into the city through this gate in front of me. As I entered the Via Delorosa and walked up the hill I thought about loss and demise and the end. It is the way of the cross here. It is the way of us all here. We all lose what we held dear. It is a most unsettling reality. We all lose our childhood. We all lose our adolescence. We all lose our creative power. It is the extreme loss that we prepare for in our lives. As we walk up towards Pilate's headquarters, and before we get our cross, we begin to feel the loss even more palpably than before.

What is God doing?
Where is my child?
Where is my daughter?
Where is my wife?
Where is the hope?
Who has the memory?
Why must it end like this?
Where does this road lead?

The tears are beginning to look like blood. There is nothing left. Then our own internal questions are replaced as others ask their own:

They ask him, "Are you the King of the Jews?"
They demand from him a creative sign.
They mock his very existence.
They are about to take away his life.
God is silent in the city of peace.

There is a silence that comes after someone has died. Be they a five year old, a seventeen year old, or a thirty-six year old mother of two. The silence is not particular to men or women, young or old. The silence is deafening to those who know it. I have sat in that silence with so many people. On the Good Fridays of our lives, the silence of the grave is on us as we all wonder "why" together.

IX

Women of the Resurrection

And when the Sabbath was past, Mary Magdalene, and Mary the mother of James, and Salome, bought spices, so that they might go and anoint him. And very early on the first day of the week they went to the tomb when the sun had risen. And they were saying to one another, "Who will roll away the stone for us from the door of the tomb?" And looking up they saw that the stone was rolled back, for it was very large. And entering the tomb, they saw a young man sitting on the right side, dressed in a white robe; and they were amazed. And he said to them, "Do not be amazed; you seek Jesus of Nazareth, who was crucified.

He is risen,

He is not here;

See the place where they laid him."　　　　Mark 16.1-6

If you want to, you can spend the night inside the church of the Holy Sepulchre. Obviously I would want to do this. Eight of my group decided to try it in the church for a vigil of sorts. We were told the doors are locked at 9:00PM and then unlocked around 5:00AM. Spending that kind of time in almost complete solitude with Calvary and the tomb of Christ under one roof was an opportunity for reflection, prayer and revelation.

To get there, we had to walk through the old city as it was shutting down for the night. We followed narrow roads full of shops. The energy is interesting, people are winding down, and we are winding up as we are making our way to the church.

When I entered the courtyard of the church I noticed the large doors. The courtyard itself is open and cool. None of us had tried this experience before, so none of us knew what to do except move past the last tourists and go inside. That moment was decisive. We had to go, go into the unknown of the church. We had to get inside, not really sure what we would find. Our walking inside the unknown not sure of what we will find would be the first metaphor for the evening.

What we found upon arriving was a frustrated Franciscan monk who reacted to our presence with, "What! This is a joke! This is ridiculous!" Besides our eight pilgrims, thirteen others had decided to spend the night in the church. "That makes twenty-one!" he said to the air. While we waited for the doors to be shut and locked, he whispered to another monk and stood there muttering with him about the need to change the rules, have a list of names, that something must be done to prevent so many pilgrims from keeping vigil or from happening again. I stood still and looked down at the Anointing Stone said to be the place where they laid Jesus' body after he had died.

I heard them lock the doors. The monk walked away and without a backward glance said, "Have a nice prayer time."

We were free to be in the church.

This church is old. Constantine commissioned it, insisting that the church be built. That was around 326 CE. It was destroyed and rebuilt after wars and conquests of the city. It has been reoriented, as the original front door faced in the opposite direction. It seems the Greek Orthodox faithful still arrive from the original direction when they worship in the space.

The space has one main altar area, several side altar areas and then countless areas for prayer. You can go down, you can go up. You can sit and view the tomb from all angles. You can go inside the tomb to sit and pray. It is at once overwhelming and simple.

My time inside the church was spent finding angles. I was curious about spots and measurements. The hill where the crosses were situated was on top of a quarry. I spent time down in the old quarry in a small chapel dedicated to St. Helena. I spent time on top, at Calvary where the crosses stood. There you can pray and sit and reflect and then touch the rock. I spent time watching the Greek Orthodox liturgy as they prayed in front of and inside of the tomb. I spent time sitting off, in back of the tomb, looking at it, wondering about it. Inspired by it. In awe of it. The space holds important landmarks of Christianity. The faithful have been gathering here since the first morning of Easter.

And here I am, and here it is, the tomb. I have preached about this place. I have been to any number of camps and vacation bible schools where a copy was built. I have read the Gospel accounts and tried to visualize it in my head. Now I was here, in the middle of the night, just here. It was a religious experience like no other I have felt, It was not transforming. It was not mind blowing. But, it had a sense of truth about it. The truth is that there is a tomb for all of us. The truth is this tomb that I was sitting near was empty. This means that the tomb waiting for all of us is empty too.

And he said to them, "Do not be amazed; you seek Jesus of Nazareth, who was crucified. He is risen, he is not here; see the place where they laid him."

This is true, He is risen. He is not there. Like all of the places I have visited in my short time here, The Holy Sepulchre is simply a place where he was once. He is risen, he is not there. Where he is, no one knows for sure. Some say he is exclusively in their church. Others say he is alive in their hearts. Still others will claim that he never rose, never died, never lived, but was a concoction, a composite of wisdom tellers. Maybe even myth. Wherever he is, his tomb is empty. When you go inside you see that for yourself. He is not there. It is empty of Jesus and full of life as each of us passes through.

The end of the story in the Gospel of Mark intrigues me. These three women want to anoint the body and so they go to the tomb early in the morning. Mary Magdalene, Mary the mother of James, and Salome. These three women are the first witnesses to the resurrection. Even though the narrative has them run away, they must have run back. Otherwise, the author would have edited them out. These three women fascinate me. They found an empty tomb when they were expecting to find it occupied. Imagine them walking up, a young girl, an adolescent and a mother. You need all three to be complete. Each represents the resurrection to me. New life. Potential to bear life. Life bearer. These three women in Mark are at the core of my faith tradition. For the resurrection to be possible, you need to have all three at the scene. While I am fascinated by them I really do not understand them. I am a male believer. I will never understand what it is to be female. I can observe, I can love, I can marry, I can witness, but I will never know.

Resurrection is like that. I can hear of it, I can read about it, I can hope for it, but I will never know it, not in my present state of living anyhow. You have to die to know resurrection. Maybe that is why Mark first remembers the women's witness of the divine action. Women are the first witnesses of divine action in the creation of organic life. Why would they not be the first witnesses of the creation of new divine life?

Sitting there in the dark listening to the sounds of worship echoing in the dome of the church, I found myself going back to the chapel over Calvary. This is a chapel I can understand. I understand suffering and dying. I have witnessed those. I am confused by the resurrection. While I proclaim it, it is still a mystery that I do not fully understand. Sitting up by Calvary I begin to have a vision of the resurrection, and now I am finally aware of my place in the story. Visions come for each pilgrim who has journeyed to this church. A vision came for me.

In my vision a child comes up to me and takes my hand. She is about five. I have met her before. She is familiar to me. I am kneeling at the hole in the floor where you can touch the rock that was the stage for the end of Jesus' life. She does not speak. I know her because I buried her. She died too young. Her death was too fast. I have a daughter like her now, and the pain her parents suffer is not one I wish for. She knows this too. She moves me quietly to the stairs and motions for me to go down. Her eyes convey the truth that this is not the place for me. Calvary's hill is empty. There is nothing there but old limestone and old icons and old lamps. New life begins with the freedom to walk away from the pain. A little child will lead them, and the first woman of the resurrection leads me. You cannot spend the night on Calvary's hill. You must go down. This child is the resurrected child of potential, the first woman of the resurrection. Thought to be dead, she is alive. She stays behind to show others this truth. She is Salome.

The Magdalene greets me by the Anointing Stone. She watches me as I set my wedding ring and my cross-ring on the stone and kneel down and pray over them. I ask God to help me live into my full potential as a husband, father, priest. Earlier in the night the stone had been anointed with perfumes and the smell is powerful and stays on my hands and rings as I get up. I look at this young woman and I recognize her. Her eyes are familiar. She is the myriad of kids I have known in my life as a youth minister. Their lives are reflected in hers. In her is confusion mixed with bravado mixed with uncertainty mixed with hope. These aspects gleam from her eyes. She was lost at one point too. She is the second woman of the resurrection. The one most of us know. She is revered and reviled and deified and demonized. She is telling me to move. She has others to tend to. Reaching out she touches my rings and quietly says, "move." Sacraments are signs of movements. You have to move; they make you move. Adolescence is movement. Sacraments and adolescences are jerky movements forward. Sacraments are imperfect timing reaching forward in living. Bread and wine, water, marriage, ordination, unction, reconciliation, confirmation are imperfections of life like puberty, pimples, hormones, facial hair, drivers' licenses, proms, and graduations. Sacraments connect us to living. They are the middle point of life, like the metamorphosis of a teenager into an adult. They are not perfect and neither is the person who receives them. The Magdalene reminds me of my true human self, my imperfection and perfection. The truth of the incarnation of Jesus is a truth found in the resurrection of Jesus, divine and human, imperfect and perfect. Rocks and poetry. The child is left at Calvary. The adolescent is anointed and matures. I move to the tomb.

As I walk to the holy tomb, I am stopped by a woman whom I recognize even more vividly. She is the third woman of the resurrection. The age peer. The confidant. The wife. She knowingly takes my arm and moves me to the front of the Holy Sepulchre. She points at it because she knows it. She suffered the pain of childbirth, and she suffered the pain of leaving children to grow on their own. She loved and was loved and had to witness love die and be reborn. She is the life maker, the life bearer, and the life sustainer. She is Mary and all women at the same time. She lets me go inside the tomb for a brief minute, a taste of what is to come. She then walks me to the door of the church and into the night air.

"You remember me, don't you?"

"Yes."

"You remember what it is you are to do, right?"

"Yes"

"Then why are you at a tomb?"

"I am not sure."

"Well, if you remember what it is you are supposed to do, and you remember me, then turn your face away and go. Living is about life, not about death. You need not worry about that at all. Creation is what creation is, and you are a part of it, so do not be afraid of it. You are a child of a living God, so live. This tomb is empty, your life is full."

She pushed me out of the church.

Suddenly I found myself walking silently with my new friends back to the College of St. George.

It was about 4:30 Sunday morning. Resurrection day. The first day of the week. The end of the work of creation and the beginning of the world. The day Christians proclaim a new life. A day we find that the tomb is empty. A day we find that our lives are full.

X

Emmaus

Luke has an account of an appearance by Jesus on the road to Emmaus. (LK 24. 13-33) In it, two disciples are walking along a road that goes to a town named Emmaus. No one really knows where that town is today. It is lost to us. Our group went looking for it and found an old Roman road that might be a road to a town that might be the town that the disciples were going towards. No one knows. It is a part of the mystery of the story.

It was pointed out to me that the two disciples were on the road to Emmaus, but stopped in a "village" where they were going. Emmaus was the road, the village was the destination. The point of that for me is that we seem to get stuck on finding Emmaus, the place, when the important piece of the story is that Jesus revealed himself to two of his disciples who were on a journey. Where the revealing is done is not as important as the revealing itself. We do this to each other often. Someone will say something wonderful happened and we will ask, "Where?"

That is not the point, really. Something wonderful has occurred. We might just enjoy the moment, instead of fixing it as a place in our minds. Something wonderful happened on an old Roman road a long time ago. A seemingly dead man appeared.

Jesus didn't appear to them on the road. They were kept from seeing him as they walked. In the story Jesus plays dumb, asking questions that had obvious answers. The two disciples marvel that Jesus was "the only visitor in Jerusalem" who didn't know what was going on in the city. Jesus then has a conversation with these two men that so intrigued them that when they get to the village where they were going they compelled Jesus to stay with them. It is later at dinner when Jesus takes, blesses, breaks, and gives the bread to these men that who he really is, is revealed.

The action of taking, blessing, breaking, giving is our Eucharistic action. It is also the request we make of God. We ask God to take our lives, bless them, mold them, and then give them to the world. It is our apostolic response to the amazing faith tradition that we have inherited. We are more than our Eucharistic feasts. We are more than our liturgies, and we are more than our places. We are people of risk and courage. We ask the God of the universe to use us, to reveal to us ways that we can serve, to take our lives and set them apart for the mission to heal and feed the world.

We heal and feed the world in many ways. How we do that is up to each one of us. Each of us is called to find where we are best able to serve. There is no one prescription that is going to be written or taught that has not already been written or taught. Each one of us has within us the ability to look around and decide. The point is to start looking around. The work begins when we open our eyes to the world around us and start healing and feeding. This can be in Gaza, or Jerusalem, or Houston, or Del Rio. I do not think that God cares where and how, but I do think that God cares that we go and do.

The story of the road to Emmaus implies that we leave Jerusalem. The story suggests that we walk out of it and then be prepared for Jesus to come walking along side of us. The story suggests that we should be prepared to understand that Jesus is going to keep going on up ahead of us. We will always be wanting more. This is the mystery of our faith: we are never satisfied, but always full.

As Christians we will never be satisfied where we are; we will always be restless, ready and looking for ways to serve the world. Yet, we will always be full. We will always have enough resources, energy, money, gumption to get the job done.

Once we set our souls onto the altar and ask God to enter in, then we have begun the journey. Suddenly without realizing it, we are walking on that road. We are telling the story of Jesus to strangers, inviting them to eat with us, listening to them and being normal people around a normal meal. Once we set ourselves on the normalcy of the situation, then Christ is revealed. When it becomes normal, everyday behavior for us to heal and feed, when our response is natural and not contrived, we suddenly become Christlike in our worldview. We become normal like Christ. It was normal for Jesus to feed five thousand people. It was normal for him to heal the sick. It was normal for him to look at the powers of the day and question whether or not they had it right. Normal. And we seek the same. It is normal for us to live our lives as Christians. Normal to take the servants' role. Normal to act out of forgiveness. Normal to find the lost and the blind and the lame and bring them into communion with God. It is this normalcy that I am going for, because in the normalcy, the extraordinary occurs.

It was a normal road, to a forgotten town, two thousand years ago. The road is gone, but the desire to have our lives used by God still burns. So we pray that Jesus will join us, will stop in our lives and take them, bless them, mold them and give them to the world. The road is still walked today. We are all on that same road when we live into our baptismal vows and reach out through the dark to bring others to the light. It is our normal duty. And we do it gladly.

Each step of our lives is pilgrimage. Journey. We are tethered to the places where the events unfolded, but those places are only for us to visit, not for us to stay. The place where we go on our journey is into the lives of each other. We cannot stay on Calvary, we cannot stay at the Anointing Stone, and we cannot stay at the tomb. We must go. We must go into the lives of each other, into community. God came into our lives through the life of Jesus of Nazareth. We go into the lives of each other through Jesus of Nazareth. The common point for us to know God is through the life of Jesus of Nazareth. However we articulate that faith, the place we end up in is a living place among the people of God. While on pilgrimage we walk. We walk with someone and in that walk the Christ is revealed.

This revelation is what I believe the Great Commission is all about. Christ revealed it to the disciples. The disciples revealed it to their world. Each generation has revealed it, tended to it, shared it and also revealed it again in their own time. The world's history finds you and me now. It is our turn. We now walk the road to Emmaus, and we now seek the living God. We tell others what we saw on the road. We keep the story alive. We fill the empty places with hope.

Epilogue

Being Empty

Let the same mind be in you that was in Christ Jesus, who, though he was in the form of God, did not regard equality with God as something to be exploited, but emptied himself, taking the form of a slave, being born in human likeness. And being found in human form, he humbled himself and became obedient to the point of death—even death on a cross.

Philippians 2.5-8

I pray that you may have the power to comprehend, with all the saints, what is the breadth and length and height and depth, and to know the love of Christ that surpasses knowledge, so that you may be filled with all the fullness of God.

Ephesians 3.17-19

I am asked to take people places. Ten years ago I was hired to drive a holy man out into the hill country to meet a wealthy woman who wanted to start a spirituality center. The man was nationally known for his work in spirituality and contemplative prayer. I picked him up at his hotel in Austin, and we began our trip west into the hill country of Texas.

As we drove along, I nervously tried to find a common topic for conversation.

"I have tried contemplative prayer," I said, "but I am too much of an extrovert to sit still for that long." He looked ahead, watching the road.

"It takes practice," he replied.

A longer than is comfortable for me moment of silence occurred.

"How long have you been ordained?" he asked me.

"About a year." I replied.

Another moment of quiet as the city blended out of view and the hill country began to take focus. He spoke up,

"You know, the Buddhists have a saying about prayer: the less you try to pray the more you are praying."

"Makes sense," I said.

The road moved along some more. I fiddled with the air conditioning. Breaking the silence I said,

"We have a singer/songwriter in Texas named Ray Wylie Hubbard who sings a song with a line that says, 'Buddha wasn't Christian, but Jesus would have made a good Buddhist.' "

"That is probably true." He replied.

"Do you like your ministry?" He asked.

"Yes," I said, "but I am still learning, seminary doesn't really prepare you for the realities of the parish. I still have more to figure out. My first year was a hard one. I made the Bishop mad early on. Happens. Still, you know, I am not dead yet."

Beat. And then under his breath I heard,

"Bring out your dead!" he said in a singsong voice.

"I'm not dead." I replied.

"'Ere, he says he's not dead." He went on.

"Yes he is." I quoted.

"I'm not." He quoted.

"He isn't." I quoted again.

"Well, he will be soon, he's very ill." He quoted in a deadpan British accent.

"I'm getting better." I quoted in a high voice.

"No you're not, you'll be stone dead in a moment." He quoted in his best John Cleese.

"Well, I can't take him like that. It's against regulations." We said together as we laughed out loud.

For the next ninety miles my holy passenger and I swapped "Monty Python and the Holy Grail" movie lines and laughed all the way.

We have such a strange reaction to the holy. We want to revere holiness and holy people and I think we should. People and objects that are set aside to honor God should be revered. They serve a holy purpose, connecting the people around them to the divine. Usually, in the presence of a holy person, we forget the holy part of us, thinking that someone or something is more holy than ourselves. And that is not true. Humans are holy because they are human. God made us in the divine image. We need not look any further for the holiness of God than at each other. There, in those eyes, there is the Holiness of God. To discount this fact is to discount God.

The purpose of a holy person is to help us cut through those things that bind us, trap us, and keep us stuck in place. Too much of the time, we offer our reverence at the expense of ourselves. A truly holy person will laugh, and help others to laugh. The holy man in the my car took me out of the false pretense of trying to look like I knew what I was talking about and set me into a place where I could laugh a little more. In a moment of trading movie lines he helped me to discover that I am not dead yet. I have more life to lead. My troubles are temporary. Until I do die, I should live.

We fill our lives with noise, thinking that the noise will cover the silence of the grave. We use our relationships and our careers as buffers to the silence. All too easily we allow ourselves to be too busy to live, to think, to pray or to laugh. We run from appointment to appointment, assignment to assignment, diaper to diaper, homework to homework in some mad dash to quell the whisper of our demise. We stutter about our worthiness in front of the throne of God, quickly running down the list of all that we have done to be credible to the creator. We grovel in the wrong direction, listing the accomplishments on our heavenly curriculum vitae; "two kids, good job, generous to all, dependable, loyal, forthright, studious, admittedly sinful, but always apologetic, straight A's." When all God wants us to do is calm down, enjoy the ride and the conversation. Maybe even laugh.

A Catholic priest acquaintance once told me that he believed that when we die and go to heaven God will ask us questions, simple questions, as we enter the holy realm, "Did you enjoy it? I made it for you. Did you like it? What did you think about the sunrises? The oceans? Dogs? Each other? I am curious to know, as it was all for you."

I have a fable I have told on Easter Sundays and at funerals. It is uncomplicated really, but I wonder about the Jesus in the tomb. I wonder about him lying there right after he was resurrected. I wonder what thoughts were going on in his head while he is in that space. There is no light inside the tomb. It is dark. The tomb is hewn into a rock, so it is humid, not cold. I wonder if he thinks about the last week of his life and the weirdness of his parade into Jerusalem. Does he remember the Temple, and the moneychangers? Does he remember Judas and the arresting guards? Does he think about the jeering crowds?

104

His mother? His friends? What does the Son of God think about after he is resurrected and before the stone is rolled away? What does a resurrected person feel? What sort of divine power is coursing through his body? Sitting up, the linen shroud falling down to his waist, I believe the Prince of Peace, the Lamb of God, the King of Kings and Lord of Lords, the carpenter from Galilee, the one who saved all of humanity, the first thing he does as he stretches into that new resurrection day, I believe he laughs.

I see Jesus in the dark of the tomb, before the stone is rolled away, and before he sees the women, right before the Angel gets there, I see Jesus laughing. Jesus is laughing to himself and saying, "What was all of that about?" Then I see him look around in the dark trying to get his bearings, comically stumbling off of the shelf where he had been laid. Standing up and looking into the dark room, the power of God coursing through his body, the moment of time and space and holiness all coalesced into this one being, I see Jesus fidgeting in his new life and after a few moments saying to the air, "the joke is on you death, the joke is on you." The stone is rolled away from all of our graves forever.

The tomb is empty; it is now a holy place, but it is an empty holy place. There is nobody there. Pilgrims come to see where it is and to pray beside it, or in it, but it is empty. Jesus left it two thousand years ago. He stepped out of the tomb and into our lives telling us that we are not dead, and that we have some work to do before we die. Our work is to empty ourselves of our business and pretension and to look at the world that God has made with empty eyes, fresh eyes, and open eyes. The way for us after the empty tomb, the pilgrimage we all embark on is one to find fullness. Fullness of life. We have full but empty lives, and we seek to be empty in order to fill our lives with the fullness of God.

Good pilgrims drop things as they walk. They drop the luggage, the things. Pilgrims drop careers and false obligations. Pilgrims walk along dropping ego, self-importance, noise. As a pilgrim walks she leaves her self-made identity along the road. As a pilgrim walks he finds new clothes to wear. As pilgrims walk the total being is remade as they approach holiness. Fear is replaced with the freedom to laugh. As a pilgrim walks he laughs. Upon his return he looks absurd to the world. His new clothes do not fit; he is in some ways unrecognizable. When pilgrims return they are empty, having exhausted their energy dropping off the things that they or someone else prescribed as right. When a pilgrim returns, they are full of the light and laughter and God. Because the tomb is empty, the joke is on death—there is no one there.

I am not sure what happens next. Pilgrims return and real life is still there. The temptation to put the old self back on, like a comfortable old shirt, is strong. That is the truth and the lie, the paradox of metanoia, the paradox of the new. The old looks so familiar, but it is a lie. The old is not the truth; it is the past, the way things were, not the way things are. Life's journey is about change, and growth, and maturity. Life's journey leads us to a tomb, but the revelation to us from our pilgrimage is that the tomb is also a part of the whole, not the end. What happens next is anybody's guess, but what happens for me is that when I am confronted with the Holy, and reminded to laugh, then I better do that. If I have reached a place in my career or my relationships where nothing is funny, and sarcasm is my lead, then I have forgotten the empty tomb, and I need to repent.

In my repentance I need a ride with a monk on a cold October day. I need Justina, and Masada, and Galilee. I need a bus ride to Bethlehem. I need the Via Delorosa and the Mount of Olives. I need fireworks in the middle of the day. I need to remember myself. I need to remember Camp Allen, healing, peace, the spirit of God. I need to remember the women of the resurrection. I need to remember to find Emmaus. I need to remember that holy man in my car that cold February day. I need to remember that I am not dead yet. And neither are you.

We are not dead yet; we have more life to lead. We are full of new life, new ideas, and new energy. The pilgrimage is just beginning. The stone is rolled away, and Jesus gets out of the tomb and moves forward, and so do we. We are still on the journey, still on the tour, still in wonder at the holy sites we see. Only now the holy sites we visit are even more divine than the city of peace. The holy sites we see are the images of God all around us in the creation and in the faces of those we love. The holy sites we see are inside of us, in our hearts. The most holy and profound site we posses is our created self. The pilgrimage now is internal. The journey now takes our empty selves and fills us with the fullness of God. We are not dead. The tomb is empty and we are full.

The call is to enjoy the journey.

So this is not the end; it is the beginning.

Acknowledgments

Many thanks to the people of St. Mark's who supported me on the journey, especially Shelley Marmon, Stephen O'Connor and Melanie Suhr. Thank you to the Diocese of Texas and its Continuing Education Program. Many thanks to the College of St. George, Jerusalem. The Very Rev. Dr. Stephen W. Need, Dean. Thank you to the Rev. Dr. Andrew Mayes for encouraging us to keep vigil in the Church of the Holy Sepluchre. Thank you to The Venerable Lois Symes, who healed me. Thank you to The Rev. Mark Brown, SSJE for his guidance. Thank you to The Rt. Rev. Allen Bartlett, Jr. retired, for the scholarship.

I will always be grateful for my thirty-three college classmates, and for my back of the bus companions Justin Gammond, Anna Noon and Caitlin Osborne.

I owe a debt of gratitude to Susan Bussey, Ph.D., Nancy Ford, Ph.D., and Andy Williams. Thanks also to Inida Chumney-Hancock, Jill Knobloch, and Dave Thompson.

Finally, to Allison, Henry and Catherine who keep me full of love and empty of doubt.

The Women of the Resurrection

In September 2001 Keri died at home of breast cancer. She was beloved by her husband and her perfect children. She fought the good fight in the face of a complicated disease.

In Janaury 2002 Elizabeth died unexepectedly. She was almost five. Her life was short by years but wonderful in her living. She will forever be missed by her parents and those who loved her.

In July 2002 Kelly died tragically in a car wreck on her way to be a camp counselor. She loved to dance. She was interested in becoming a priest. There is a poem she wrote that inspires. It is set at the end of a trail dedicated to her memory at Camp Allen.

They are the women of the resurrection. This book and my ministry are dedicated to them. Their parents and loved ones are some of the most resilient people I have ever met.

They know the tomb is empty; they know of resurrection. There is hope in their loss. I am grateful to have been a priest with them and their families. I am grateful they found me that night in the church.